Sarah Eberle's
Psalm 23 Garden

Design tips for a calm green space

Bible Society
Stonehill Green
Westlea
Swindon SN5 7DG
biblesociety.org.uk

First published 2021 by The British and Foreign Bible Society.

ISBN: 978-0-564-04967-7

Design and production by Bible Society Resources Ltd, a wholly owned subsidiary of The British and Foreign Bible Society.

BSRL/1.8M/2021
Printed in Great Britain

Foreword

My love for landscape goes back to my early childhood. Charmed by the Devon country hedge banks, awed by the moody personality of the sea and inspired by soft light and shadows, my future was set.

As a landscape architect and a garden designer, I am fortunate to work on landscapes and gardens from the tiny to the vast. Although the Psalm 23 Garden is diminutive in size, it is huge in stature and, especially in the context of Covid-19, relevant to us all, as our need to engage with nature becomes increasingly important.

The Psalm 23 Garden aims to engage our emotions, to be a place of contemplation and spiritual renewal, portraying an ultimate destination that makes the trouble of life's journey worthwhile. The selection of weathered rock reflects the wear and tear that shapes us during life's varied journey.

Beyond our cultures and experience, we all share a historical relationship with nature. Building gardens together as a community breaks down loneliness, and builds friendships and common interest.

Growing together allows us to escape to nature and even grow food while soothing troubled minds – increasingly relevant and important in a stressful world.

I hope this book will inspire you with fresh ideas about what you could do in your own garden, or to take part in creating a Psalm 23-inspired community garden. Enthusiasm is more important than expertise, and, as we know, gardening can be transformative.

So many of our important horticulturalists became passionate about gardening from time spent with a parent or a grandparent who gardened and grew flowers and edible plants. Gardening develops patience and dialogue and teaches us about success and failure, perhaps making us more tolerant human beings.

I have yet to meet anyone who, although initially a reluctant gardener, has not become addicted, with the garden becoming a place to lose your mind and find your soul.

I can be quite bossy, so my advice to you is JUST DO IT! You will not regret it, I promise. A familiar cry is, 'I don't know where to start.' The answer is, just start, anywhere: a pot on the windowsill, a window box, a small part of a garden. There are help groups if that is what you need to get you going. The Royal Horticultural Society is a charity that does an enormous amount in support of community initiatives.

Do not be blinded by the science. The greatest pleasure is in having a go,

whether at a steady, well-considered pace, or as an exciting adventurous escapade. If you have no garden, then joining a community garden to help build or maintain one can be an important and rewarding personal and relational step. Plant flowers or shrubs, grow vegetables and provide some space for quiet enjoyment – and if it works for you, it works.

I hope that this book and the story of the Psalm 23 Garden may in some small way inspire you to start on this journey of love, excitement, aching muscles, and utter contentment.

Good luck!

Sarah Eberle
Designer

Acknowledgements

Creating a garden for the RHS Chelsea Flower Show requires the commitment and skill of a huge team of people. This book is part of that endeavour. The tone has been set by Sarah Eberle, a designer with real vision for this garden and the ability to express it, who's also been enormous fun to work with. We've spent hours planning, but laughing too, despite the challenges of the last few years. When looking for someone to build your garden, the best man for the job is Mark Gregory, who implements the vision and brings it to reality. We are hugely thankful to have been working with both of them, and I still pinch myself that we have been.

Our thanks also go to the team at the Royal Horticultural Society for all their support.

Behind the scenes are those at Bible Society who've worked hard through all the handbrake turns that the coronavirus pandemic has thrown at us: Ryan Anderson, Debbie Clifford, Elaine Dony, Richard Franklin, Esther King, Andy Knight, Susannah Mansfield, Pete Nichol, Mel O'Sullivan, Mike Otter, Phil Rodgers, Adam Smith, Luke Walton and Elaine Young.

And none of this would have been possible without Fran Clifton, James Greig and Whitestone Media.

This book was the brainchild of Paul Williams, but wouldn't have been possible without the skills of editors Mark Woods and Lisa Cherrett, designer Emily Heskins, and photographers Clare Kendall, Alex Baker, James Greig, Scot Openshaw and Pete Wooding.

We'd also like to thank Jackie, Graham, Jacky, Julie, Dave, Eunice, Janet and Kiri for sharing their experiences of Psalm 23. Finally, thanks go to St Mary's Church in Tadley, for creating a Psalm 23-inspired community garden during lockdown and allowing us to tell their story.

I hope that I, too, have been able to make a contribution to something that you will love and find useful both in your community and in your back garden. As a team, we wish you well with your Psalm 23-inspired gardens.

Hazel Southam
Author and Psalm 23 Garden project manager

Introduction

Why should Bible Society sponsor a garden at the RHS Chelsea Flower Show? And why pick Psalm 23?

Gardening is a theme that runs through the whole of the Bible. The first book of the Bible, Genesis, describes Adam as a gardener. The people of ancient Israel were farmers and agriculturalists, living close to the soil. The love story of the Song of Solomon takes place in a garden; Jesus was betrayed in a garden; and the whole Bible ends in a garden city, in the book of Revelation. So, for us, the connections are built in.

Bible Society also believes that the Bible is a book for everyone, not just for the Church. It inspires, comforts, mystifies and provokes. Throughout our nation's history, it's been the bedrock of our culture. Part of our mission is to find ways it can continue to speak today.

Psalm 23 – 'The Lord is my shepherd' – is one of the best-known and best-loved passages in the Bible. We know it not just from funerals and school assemblies, but from sitcoms (like *The Vicar of Dibley*), films (it's in *Titanic*, *Pale Rider* and *Rooster Cogburn*, among others) and even rap (Coolio, Tupac, Eminem and Kanye all quote from it). We all recognise phrases like 'green pastures' and 'the valley of the shadow of death'.

So, with the help of top designer Sarah Eberle, we offered another take on Psalm 23 and turned it into a garden. This book comes out of that experience. Sarah's shared her expertise on garden design, and the

photographs by Clare Kendall make it visually stunning. But Psalm 23 has a spiritual message as well. It speaks of God as a shepherd who cares for his flock, and as a host who cares for his guests. It celebrates the 'green pastures and quiet waters' that give us joy; it's honest and realistic about the 'dark valleys' we go through on our way through life; it speaks of our need for help and deliverance – and it ends with hope for the future. In just a few verses it reflects the whole Bible story.

The psalm is a gift to us from God, and we're delighted to be able to share it with you.

The LORD Is My Shepherd
A Psalm of David

The LORD is my shepherd; I shall not want.
　　He makes me lie down in green pastures.
He leads me beside still waters.
　　He restores my soul.
He leads me in paths of righteousness
　　for his name's sake.

Even though I walk through the valley of the shadow of death,
　　I will fear no evil,
for you are with me;
　　your rod and your staff,
　　they comfort me.

You prepare a table before me
　　in the presence of my enemies;
you anoint my head with oil;
　　my cup overflows.
Surely goodness and mercy shall follow me
　　all the days of my life,
and I shall dwell in the house of the LORD
　　for ever.

Psalm 23

English Standard Version (ESV)

Sarah Eberle

How the design works

The starting point for the design of the garden is the visual nature of Psalm 23. The psalm takes you on the journey of life, through a landscape. You can visualise it, just by reading. So, the garden needed to show elements of that journey, as well as the final destination.

When people look at the garden, I hope they'll say the psalm to themselves and call to mind the elements from it that they can see, such as the 'still waters'. The garden works on an emotional level, and it should engage people's emotions as they look at it.

How do you depict the valley of the shadow of death? Here, I've used rock to create a difficult, challenging journey through the garden. To get to the garden's destination, you have to climb over rocks. In life, everybody goes through difficult times – as we all have recently – and this is what the psalm is talking about. Life isn't smooth. There

are problems, fears and, as we now know, pandemics.

After the difficult journey comes the place of destination. It has a feeling of calm, a place where you can be embraced by your surroundings. This is the sense that I took from the psalm. So, the garden is designed to be a place that feels like a sanctuary, a haven, where you are protected from harm.

How is this achieved? It's done partly through the use of water. We know that water is incredibly calming, particularly if we are struggling with mental health issues. But to create a sense of a calm destination, the water feature has to be

right. It has to be placed correctly within the overall structure of the garden, and it has to be an appropriate size. All of this gives balance, which in itself is calming.

The plants in the garden also help to create the feeling of the psalm. Everything is very soft, texturally. For instance, I've used grasses, ferns and members of the cow parsley family, which are all soft. So, the overall feeling of the planting is that the plants could hug you. Planting choices are about what you leave out as well as what you include. For example, however beautiful roses are, you wouldn't want to be hugged by a rose, as they have thorns.

How the design works: Sarah Eberle

The trees also play a significant role in creating the feel of the garden. Trees offer protection under their canopies, giving the traveller a place where they can shelter and look around them, but not be seen. Trees are significant to all of us. Who doesn't have a favourite tree? The trees in the Psalm 23 Garden are also trees that naturally belong in this landscape, weathered trees that have lived through life's difficulties themselves. So the trees contribute a lot.

> "
> *The whole place has a sense of calm, which I hope will enable people to reflect on their own lives. It's the kind of garden that I trust people will be drawn back to again and again.*
> "

The Lord is my shepherd;
I shall not want.

PSALM 23.1

Reflection

PSALM **23** VERSE **1** | THE LORD IS MY SHEPHERD

Shepherds in ancient Israel were heroes – at least if they were good at their jobs. The landscape wasn't tamed, as it is in much of the UK. There were dangerous predators including lions and bears, and in mountainous areas the terrain could be perilous too. Protecting and caring for the sheep was a job for someone who was mentally and physically tough. A shepherd might cover long distances on foot and live largely out of doors, at times with little food or sleep.

David, who's traditionally thought to have written this psalm, had been a shepherd himself. When he said to God, 'You, Lord, are my shepherd', he was speaking out of his own experience – and admitting something deeply personal. He was saying that, tough and wily as he was, God was even stronger. David was used to being in control, but he knew there were problems he couldn't solve. The protector and carer needed protection and care.

We often like to think we've got everything sorted. Psalm 23 tells us that it's OK if we haven't. Right at the beginning of the psalm, we're told: don't worry. We probably aren't as tough as we think we are, but that's all right: God is there to guard us and guide us, and dig us out of the holes we find ourselves in. As we've seen over the last year, even the toughest shepherd needs a shepherd.

Jackie's story

'I've been spending a lot of time in my garden during the coronavirus pandemic. I find gardening very therapeutic. To be in contact with nature, with God's creation, is important. If I have a bad day, I dig. It's very good therapy.

'I've been dealing with ten years of neglect in the garden and have started a vegetable patch. I sacrificed half of the lawn and am growing beetroot, radishes, spinach, beans and peas – whatever seeds I could get.

'When lockdown began, our Bishop suggested that we all read Psalm 23 every day. The discipline of that has been good. It's been hugely helpful.

'I've been reading Psalm 23 and thinking about gardening. When my seedlings came up through the soil, I thought, "My cup runneth over." I felt God's goodness coming through the earth.

'The whole idea of having one's head anointed with oil, and that goodness and mercy will follow me through the valley of the shadow of death, has been hugely helpful.

'If you dwell on a text like this, you will hear or read what you need to know. That's felt very powerful over these last months. It's kept us going, really.'

> *Psalm 23 has helped me through the pandemic*

Sarah Eberle

Every garden can have a tree

It really is true to say that every garden, no matter how small, can have a tree. Trees create a beautiful quality of light and shade. They give us somewhere to retreat to. And they are nature's sieves, helping to clean the air of pollution and carbon dioxide, and releasing oxygen for us to breathe.

Every garden can have a tree: Sarah Eberle

They provide a canopy and a haven, not just for us but for wildlife too. A tree will be a magnet and home for birds. But the biodiversity that trees bring is far greater than that which can be seen with the naked eye. A recent scientific study found that Britain's native oak trees are home to, or used by, an astonishing 2,300 different species: 38 species of birds, 229 mosses, 716 lichens, 1,178 invertebrates and 31 mammals.

Not many of us can plant an oak tree at home – you need a lot of space – but we can all plant a tree, and so add to the habitats and biodiversity of our gardens.

So, what do you choose? First, look for a multi-stemmed tree that's shaped like an umbrella, such as amelanchier or birch. For most back gardens, you want something on a human scale that you can walk underneath, but also lets you see the canopy. You don't want to be staring at the tree's trunk all the time.

Second, think about the volume of the tree and make sure it fits with what's around it and the size of the garden that it will be in. You want to create a sense of balance in your garden. Choosing the right tree helps achieve this. So, avoid impulse buys!

Third, think about the soil and aspect where the tree will be planted. Some trees do better on chalk, others on clay, so know your soil. You're looking for a hardworking tree that will be tough enough to endure all weathers and the threats posed by climate change.

The fourth thing to consider is the colour and habit of your tree. Think about the colour of the leaves and bark. Will they go with things that are already in your garden? If you're starting a garden from scratch, you have the great joy of choosing your tree, or trees, first, and then adding the supporting cast of tiers of plants under and around it: shrubs, herbaceous perennials and bulbs, even climbers going through it. But thinking about your tree as part of a cohesive whole is important.

Once you've whittled down your long list to a short list of likely contenders, what should you do next? The answer is simple: go as big as you can afford. You want to enjoy this tree during your lifetime and that's unlikely to happen if you buy a £5 tree from a supermarket.

So, research local specialist tree nurseries, visit them and talk to them about your short list. Look at the trees that are options for you, and take advice. You won't regret it.

Finally, buy British-grown trees. Climate change has added to the number of diseases among trees. We can all help to prevent diseased trees entering the UK by buying trees that have been grown here.

Reflection

PSALM **23** VERSE **2** | HE RESTORES MY SOUL

A running theme in the Bible is the idea of God as the creator. Right at the beginning, in the book of Genesis, there's a picture of a world at peace with itself. The refrain in Genesis 1 is, 'And God saw that it was good.' No one dies, and everything is in harmony. It's this kind of picture that's reflected here in Psalm 23. It celebrates the goodness of creation.

The creation stories are very rich. They're expressions of how the writers believed the world ought to be. And at the end of the story in Genesis 1 there's a 'sabbath', when God 'rested from all his work'.

Sabbath has sometimes become a list of things you're not allowed to do. But it really means not having to labour 24/7 to stay alive – having time to lie down in green pastures and walk beside still waters.

Human beings weren't designed to work without ceasing. It's leisure time that produces music, art and poetry. And it's because we aren't working all the time that we have space for other people in our lives. We need that time if we're going to flourish, with good friends and healthy relationships.

Many of us aren't good at resting. If we're at school, it's all about results. If we're at work, it's about productivity. Even when we aren't working, there's pressure on us to hit the gym and exercise or hit the shops and consume. It's not good for us.

We're part of God's creation – made to rest as well as work.

He makes me lie down in green pastures.
He leads me beside still waters.
He restores my soul.

PSALM 23.2

Kiri's story

Psalm 23 gives me a sense of the wraparound love of God

'I used to love cross-country running. I ran every morning. I picked up an injury, or at least, I thought that was what happened. It affected my posture and caused me a lot of pain. I thought that I was going to have to live with on–off pain.

'Then, in 2018, I was diagnosed with ankylosing spondylitis, a form of joint inflammation that affects the spine. It's a chronic, degenerative condition. In some ways it was a relief to have a diagnosis. Other things fell into place, like mental fog and fatigue. But it was also heartbreaking, because it is incurable and tends to be progressive, although there are drugs that hold it at bay.

'On the days when I struggle, it can be difficult to remember my PIN or a meeting. Psalm 23 is so well-known that it's one of the things I can remember and recite back. A while back, I started reading different translations of it and found The Message version. It was revelatory. Different things jumped out at me.

'It refers to "Death Valley". When I'm in a flare, when things are painful and difficult, it feels like I'm in this world but going through something private and dark at the same time. Things that normally seem easy, like tying my shoelaces, get really difficult.

'This version also talks about God reviving "my drooping head". That's so meaningful for me because standing straight is something I now struggle with. So that's really poignant.

'Psalm 23 is a safe retreat. The hope held in it helps me to know that I'm going to get through this situation. I keep going back to this psalm. I read it at least once a week. Psalm 23 makes me feel taken care of.

'I got married a couple of years ago. Before that, when I lived on my own, I would sometimes cry by myself alone in my house. I'm not someone who finds it easy to call up a friend to cry. But I felt I could cry out the verses of Psalm 23 and that there was rest.

'I'm still coming to terms with my diagnosis. Immediately after it, I felt very low. I'm managing that a lot better now – I'm much more attuned to my symptoms. But I'm still working through my thoughts about disability and what that means.

'Psalm 23 meets me where I am and helps me to deal with the present. It gives me a sense of the wraparound love of God and his nurturing, and that's comforting.'

Sarah Eberle

How to add water to your garden

Water has many attributes. It's cooling, bringing down the air temperature and often our own temperatures too! Just the sound of water can be calming, and can disguise traffic noise if you live on a busy road.

How to add water to your garden: Sarah Eberle

Using water in a garden creates a focal point, a place for reflection. And if you use something like a large black bowl, you will have physical reflections too, which is beautiful. Still water creates reflections; moving water doesn't.

Another thing to consider when adding water to a garden is the scale. Your water feature needs to be in proportion to the rest of the garden. If you have three-quarters of an acre with a small water tub, it will feel out of proportion.

Then think about where the water will go and what it will do. Is it there for its sound, movement or reflection? This will help you decide on the kind of water feature that you want. Think about your location too. Choose a water feature that fits in with the styling and location of your garden, whether urban, rural or suburban. There's a style and an appropriate water feature for everywhere, but think

about your choices. Whatever your choice, water will draw wildlife into your garden, and not just the birds and small mammals that you might expect. Bees, for instance, love to come and drink water as they forage for nectar and pollen. Still water will both attract and help them.

A water feature, like a sculpture, is something to be enjoyed, so place it within the eyeline of where you sit. If you hide your water feature out of sight, you won't be able to enjoy it while you're having a cup of tea in the garden. Treat it like a sculpture, and ensure that you can see it from where you are sitting.

Rather like trees, it's important not to impulse buy or simply buy the cheapest thing from the internet. Have a look at what other people have done, read magazines and check out gardening books for ideas. Then, when

you're inspired, think about what will work realistically, in your garden.

There are two important things to remember with water. First, a water feature, or pond, will need gardening just like any other part of your garden. You may not be doing it with a trowel or fork, but it will need maintenance and care.

The second thing is that not every garden absolutely must have water. Water is both a delight and a risk to children. If you're creating a pond, for example, in a garden where children play, put a steel mesh an inch beneath the surface of the water. It won't be seen, but it will help prevent accidents.

If you do decide to include water in your garden, you could keep a record of the wildlife that it draws in, both night and day. You'll see quite quickly that you are not the only beneficiary of water in the garden.

He leads me in paths of righteousness for his name's sake.

PSALM 23.3

Reflection

PSALM **23** VERSE **3** | PATHS OF RIGHTEOUSNESS

People who live in developed countries have more choices than ever. It's not true of everyone – many of us are still limited by circumstances – but on the whole we can choose where to live, what to eat and drink, what to wear, our jobs, our friends, our lifestyles. We can choose how to live, too. What are our values? What do we believe about right and wrong? What gives our lives meaning?

In lots of ways this freedom is a great blessing. In others, perhaps not so much. Even choice can seem oppressive, as we constantly worry about whether we've made the right decisions. Everything from an Instagram post to a menu choice becomes another hurdle to jump.

And if we're honest, we'll admit that we've often made wrong choices, about things that really matter. Sometimes we might have thought we were doing the right thing, and we weren't; at other times, we've known all along that we were wrong.

This sense of confusion and failure is in the psalmist's mind when he says that God leads him in right paths. There's a way through the wilderness; the pathways are there, if we can only learn to see them. And God leads us 'for his name's sake': his nature is to guide us and protect us.

Dave's story

'I'm a season-ticket supporter at West Bromwich Albion. You are born a fan, you don't become one. My Dad used to take me in the Sixties. Now, I take my grandson.

'The Lord's my Shepherd (Psalm 23) is what they sing whenever Albion score a goal. That's what all the fans sing.

'It's one of the most uplifting psalms in the world. Recently we got taken over by the Chinese and they put the first couple of verses around the ground underneath the bulwarks. If you went to West Bromwich Albion, you would see the first couple of verses.

'It feels wonderful when everyone sings Psalm 23. I love it. The other guys are singing because they have scored a goal. I think the Lord listens. I'm always praying that something of what they are singing might just sink in. I love the atmosphere when everyone sings Psalm 23. I think it changes something.

'I can really meet God on those terraces. I feel that we have a cloud of witnesses watching us at matches. Everyone on the terraces is an expert. I feel like God's cheering us on. Isn't that something? God is shouting from the terraces for us to hear. I think God is still calling out.

'It helps to know that the Lord is there with me.'

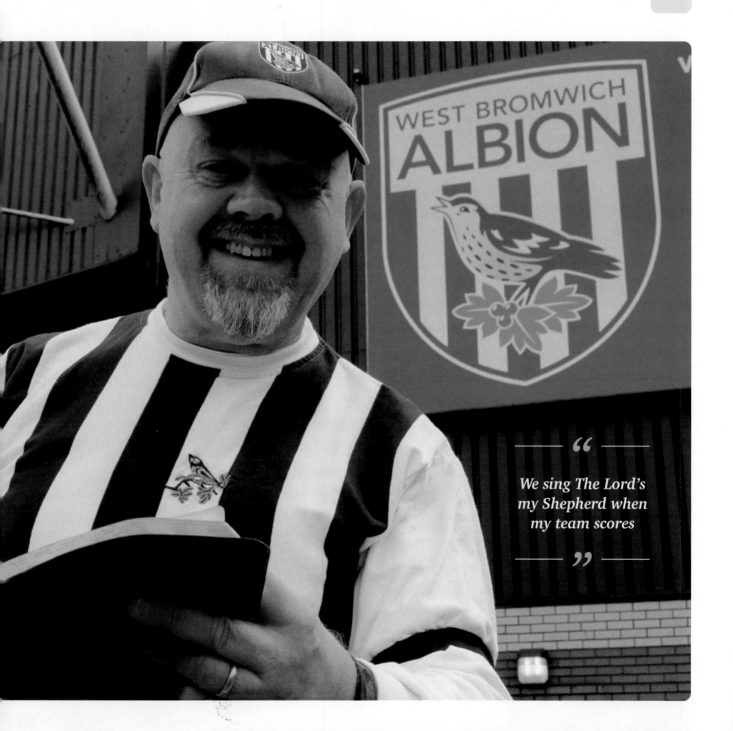

WEST BROMWICH
ALBION

> "
> *We sing The Lord's
> my Shepherd when
> my team scores*
> "

Sarah Eberle

How to use naturalistic planting

Naturalistic planting comes in many different forms and guises, but always looks natural. It looks like a natural habitat rather than a created space, and yet it's one of the most-considered and thought-through types of planting.

How to use naturalistic planting: Sarah Eberle

You can see this at work very clearly in the Psalm 23 Garden. It looks like a beautiful place that you've stumbled across on a country walk, rather than a highly curated garden.

It's quite a challenge to do, so it's more for the keen amateur or professional gardener. But there's a type of naturalistic planting that we can all try: creating a wildflower area.

According to the conservation charity Plantlife, some 97 per cent of Britain's wildflower meadows have been destroyed since the 1930s. Back then, Britain was awash with colourful, grassy meadows, rich in wildlife and beautiful to behold. Some 7.5 million acres have gone, leaving just one per cent of our countryside with this kind of habitat.

It's a tragedy that we can all help to reverse by creating wildflower areas. You can let your whole lawn go, and mow paths through it, or have longer areas of grass and wildflowers around them. Even if you've just got a window box, planting wildflowers will help.

So, how do you do it? You start in autumn when plants are going into their dormant phase. If you're going to add to your lawn, you must first weaken the tough lawn grass by letting it grow long. Then you can plant tough perennials within it.

Or you could take up your lawn and seed the ground with wildflower seeds. If you opt for this route, keep an eye out for tough plants that you don't want getting a foothold. Plants like dock and nettle are valuable native species, but they might not be what you want across what was once your lawn. If you're sowing perennial wildflower seeds such as geranium or *Leucanthemum Silene*, then autumn is the time for this job. If, however, you want to sow an annual mix, perhaps including field poppy, cornflower and corn marigold, the time to do this is in the spring, once the soil has warmed up.

It's also possible to buy wildflower turf. Companies selling turfs provide a huge variety for all different soils and aspects. So think about your soil type and the setting of the garden when you're ordering.

Try to include grasses in your meadow. They will give you something beautiful to look at in winter, they'll create a billowing structure through which other plants can grow, and their seeds will be an invaluable source of food for birds and small mammals.

Whichever route you take to creating a wildflower area, you'll be helping to redress the balance of the last 90 years of destruction – creating areas of beautiful habitat and a place of real interest that changes with the seasons and over the years.

Reflection

PSALM **23** VERSE **4** | DARK VALLEYS

Unless we're very fortunate indeed, most of us will go through dark valleys at some time in our lives – and recently all of us have been going through the dark valley of the coronavirus pandemic. Shakespeare talks about the 'heartaches and the thousand natural shocks' we face just because we're human. While we can't escape this kind of experience, sometimes these valleys take on a deeper darkness as we are overwhelmed by what we face. Life becomes bleak. We see no hope. So how can the psalmist say, 'I will fear no evil'?

There are two words in these verses that might help us. One is 'through' and the other is 'with'.

Most of us find that, however dark our personal valley might be, we don't stay in it forever. We go through it and we come out on the other side. We weren't designed to live in darkness: God wants something better for us.

And we do not go through it alone. God is with us, the psalmist says. The 'rod' of which the shepherd-poet speaks is less like a walker's pole and more like a club. It's a support, but also a weapon that can be used to defend us against evil. The shepherd-God is a rescuer, who guards us and guides us. It's no accident that Jesus describes himself as 'the good shepherd' and that one of his titles is 'Immanuel', which means 'God with us'.

We go through the valley and God is with us.

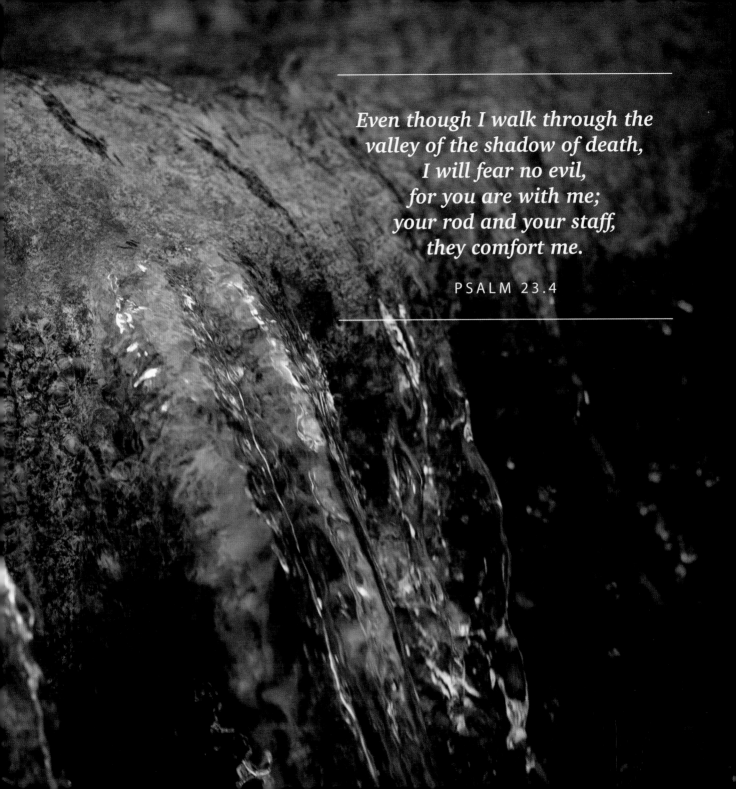

*Even though I walk through the
valley of the shadow of death,
I will fear no evil,
for you are with me;
your rod and your staff,
they comfort me.*

PSALM 23.4

My son died of cancer

Jacky's story

'My son Jon was 16 and he had terrible headaches. The doctors didn't think it was anything, but in 2002 he was diagnosed with a brain tumour. He had an emergency operation and then a year of radiotherapy and chemotherapy.

'He came out of it and seemed to be cured. He finished school and was an apprentice with the council. He had just moved into a little flat by himself when he had a five-year scan. It was the last one he was going to have. He got a phone call on the bus to say they had found something. It was 2008, and the cancer had come back. In 2010, it spread to his lymph glands.

'Psalm 23 comes into it when he was going downhill in 2012. He wasn't well enough to go to church any more. He used a wheelchair. He had a hut in the garden and we would have our own little acts of worship in there.

'That was what we were doing and that was when he came across the York Minster Choir singing The Lord is My Shepherd. He loved it. When he went into the hospice, he listened to it quite a lot and I read it to him too.

'On his last day of consciousness, when he was 26, one of the vicars came to visit and Jon told him that it was his favourite reading. There was a room in the hospice which had a window with a stream and green fields in it, like Psalm 23. The vicar read Psalm 23 and Jon said, "That was wonderful." After that, he went to sleep. It was really, really special to Jon.

'We didn't discuss it, but I'm sure it conjured up this place which was so beautiful and the Lord taking away the pain that he had. He had nothing to fear because God was with him. The banquet was right up his street as well. He could imagine that being with God was going to be rather good and it gave him strength and comfort.'

Sarah Eberle

How to use seating

A garden is a place to dally awhile, so seating is a must for all gardens. There are three kinds of seating for you to consider.

The first is formal seating for dining. You'd have this near to the house, to make it easier to go in and out with food and drink. The second is the sort where you'd have coffee with a friend. It's more casual, and it might not be as close to the house. The third kind of seating, the really special kind, is incidental seating. This is the kind that doesn't look like seating at all. It never looks as if it was put there deliberately. It looks as if it simply belongs in the landscape and you discovered it. So it's definitely not something you'd find on a lawn. Incidental seating is tucked away in the nooks and crannies of a garden. It can be almost anything: a seat hanging from a tree, a rock, an old tree stump, a pallet that's been upcycled.

The important thing is that incidental seating gives you somewhere that feels like a secret hideaway, a place where you can escape from all the pressures of life. It's a place that allows you just

to be, to contemplate, and we all need that. So, using something that looks like it's part of the landscape – such as a tree stump, a log, or a block of local stone – is particularly effective. If it looks like it belongs, then you instantly feel relaxed, as though you've discovered a special place.

However, there's lots that you can do by recycling, which is great for all kinds of seating. Scrapyards are some of my favourite places. You never know what you might find. But when you see something that's suitable for your garden, you'll know.

This means that seating really need not be expensive. It simply has to be inviting, comfortable and appropriate for its setting.

If you think that you can only afford a few plastic chairs, think again. Plastic isn't inherently bad, but we all need to use it less. That applies to garden chairs as much as it does to food packaging. But if plastic furniture really is the right choice for you, try to find some recycled plastic chairs, or ones that are being given away on a free site. Then you can upcycle them yourself, with just a lick of paint, and turn them into something new and personal.

How to use seating: Sarah Eberle

*You prepare a table before me
in the presence of my enemies;
you anoint my head with oil;
my cup overflows.*

PSALM 23.5

Reflection

PSALM **23** VERSE **5** | A GRACIOUS HOST

Meal tables are full of meaning. They're where families sit together, where couples' eyes meet and where we enjoy life's good things. They're also where things fall apart: families row and relationships break up. It's painful to know that there are tables to which we are not invited and where we are not welcome.

The psalmist, though, pictures God as a gracious host who invites us 'in the presence of my enemies'. At a time when we may be alone, excluded and afraid, he offers us asylum and sanctuary. At a table in the wilderness, he treats us as an honoured guest.

In Jewish tradition, this psalm was written when David was facing a fight for his life. The table God prepared for him was to strengthen him for the coming battle.

Many of us face our own battles today, and we need strength too – and the divine table is a very earthly, material place. It's often in human contact, the blessings of friendship and the love of other people that we find God strengthens us. And the table is a place of welcome. In one of his parables, Jesus talks of a king who throws a party and invites the outsiders, not just the rich and respectable. In God's hospitality tent, strangers and enemies become friends.

Eunice's story

'Psalm 23 is what I always go to in the ups and downs of my life. I always hold on to it. My son used to have a lot of trouble with the police. It was theft, stupid things, breaking into cars. It was a worry for me.

'I drew comfort from Psalm 23. I would get up in the morning and continually pray it. It was saying to me that I had the Lord to hold on to. I felt that there was hope for my son because of that. Every day I would ask God to take care of everything and then I left everything in his hands. I prayed that my son would turn around one day.

'I remember one day we went to court. The judge was angry with the police for picking on my son. He said, "Why don't you leave him alone? Don't do anything else like that."

'I've seen others who were in and out of prison all the time. They had no future. Some are still the same. If my son didn't have me, relying on God, he might be like one of those boys today.

'Now, he's working in catering. He has a family – 11 children – and he's a grandfather. It's because of God.'

> "
> *My son was in trouble with the police*
> "

Sarah Eberle

How to use shade-loving plants

Shady places are becoming increasingly popular in our gardens as the climate becomes hotter. So, celebrate and work with the shady areas in your garden, whether they are under trees or shrubs, or simply against the north wall of your house. By working with what you have, you can create a garden of real beauty.

How to use shade-loving plants: Sarah Eberle

Shade is as good for many plants as it is for us. It prevents them getting 'burned' by the contrast of cool nights and then hot early morning sun. It allows them to flourish.

The key to success is picking the right plants for the right places. When working with shade, think about a woodland. It has a tall layer of trees, an understorey of shrubs and bushes, and then, frequently, spring-flowering plants and ferns.

You can transfer this principle to your garden, using shrubs such as box as an understorey beneath large trees, and then planting perennials or bulbs. Those that do best in shade will be bulbs and perennials that flower in the autumn, winter or spring, when trees (or shrubs) aren't in leaf and more light is available. You could think about corydalis, lily of the valley, anemones, snowdrops and epimediums.

It will be difficult to plant close to the roots of an established tree or a shrub. But come slightly further out, towards the edge of the canopy, and there should be enough soil and water for your plants to become established.

I always use plug plants when planting under trees. They are easier to get established in this situation, but will need regular watering until that's the case, when they can compete for water with the tree.

If you've got an area of damp shade, different plants are required. Hostas, euphorbias, astilbe, pulmonaria and primulas will all flourish in these conditions.

Deep shade can feel intimidating, but really needn't be. Again, remember the principle of woodland. Dense shade will have fewer shafts of light coming through the trees, but you can create brighter patches by judicious use of variegated plants. Something like Cornus 'White Gold' will create a splash of light in the darkness and so lift the whole area. You can use plants with glossy foliage, such as fatsia, that will mirror and reflect light.

You can even plant up against the north face of a house. There are a number of climbers and shrubs that will do well in these conditions. These include akebia and climbing hydrangea. It may surprise you to learn that you can even have roses on a north wall. Some good options are Constance Spry, The Pilgrim and Graham Thomas.

Shade in gardens is a blessing rather than a problem. Find the right plants for your soil and aspect, and you can have year-round interest in the garden because of it.

Reflection

PSALM **23** VERSE **6** | GOODNESS AND MERCY

There's a deep insight in this verse, and an inspiring hope. There are dark valleys to go through; David might have thought he deserved better from God. But he still believes that God will protect and comfort him.

However, he puts that in a very interesting way. God's goodness and mercy will 'follow' him, he says. It isn't necessarily that he will always experience these blessings all the time, but they are never far away. Even when our whole lives seem to be a vast darkness, the light is waiting to shine. One writer, Douglas MacMillan – himself a former shepherd – writes of an old Highland shepherd who imagined Goodness and Mercy as sheepdogs following the flock, ready to intervene when the sheep are in trouble, always alert for the shepherd's command.

There's also a great hope here. The psalmist says he will 'dwell in the house of the Lord for ever'. We're thankful for blessings when we face troubles today, but we still want those troubles to have an ending. The psalmist tells us that they will. The table in the presence of his enemies is a foretaste of eternity.

The Bible values life and living – Jesus told his followers he had come to give them life 'to the full'. But it also points forward, to 'a new heaven and a new earth'; at the end of the Bible, God says, 'I am making everything new.' The story of the Bible ends with hope.

*Surely goodness and mercy
shall follow me
all the days of my life,
and I shall dwell in the
house of the Lord
for ever.*

PSALM 23.6

> "
> *Psalm 23 calmed me
> when I was caving*
> "

Graham's story

'Caving was a big part of my life for many years. When you are in times of danger or extreme fear, like being on a rope hanging off a cliff, that tends to concentrate the mind.

'I had to memorise Psalm 23 at school. I especially liked the part about not being afraid. It says that there is nothing to fear. That makes me think that God is with you. So, I used to say it when I was caving.

'One time, I was caving in the UK and had entered a tunnel which started to collapse. I started to recite the 23rd Psalm and passages seemed to hold themselves up until I had just crawled out of them. It felt as if the tunnel was literally being held up.

'We never read the guide books, but that was the fun of it. When we came out of it, I read the guide book and it said, "The entrance will collapse." We were idiots.

'There were other situations too. We took a team down a pull-through drop. You walk up the mountain with the rope and take the rope down with you, so you can't go back up. We had come down the first pitch and were crawling down a coffin level [named after its shape] and we heard a flood pulse, which is when it's raining and it goes straight into the system.

'We had to get out. We literally escaped with our lives, but there was a team that died just behind us. That was one of those times [when I relied on Psalm 23]. I couldn't see any floor before me; all I could see was big water. As soon as I went under the water, it was that strong, I couldn't hold on. I was floating through the stream, but I seemed to be rushed to the ledge at the side. I don't know how that happened. I had been saying the Psalm before I went down.

'The Bible was my dirty secret. I had my Bible in my bag so my friends wouldn't see me.

'I was reckless, but there were also moments of fear. Psalm 23 calmed me each time so I didn't panic.'

Sarah Eberle

How to create your own community garden

Feel enthused? You can create a community garden inspired by Sarah Eberle's Psalm 23 Garden. It just takes four simple steps.

Plant a tree

Every garden – no matter how small – can have a tree. It creates a focal point for the eye, provides shade, gives height and brings in wildlife. This will create the illusion that your space is bigger than it is, as the tree creates a visual bridge between your garden and the environment around it.

Look around you to see what kind of trees do well in your local area. This will be about the type of soil you have and the aspect of the land you're planting on.

Then buy British, and go for the largest tree that you can afford. That way, you'll enjoy it, rather than waiting many years for it to grow.

Water

Water adds a sense of relaxation and tranquillity to any garden, however small or large. It's a real pleasure simply to sit and listen to the sound of the water and watch the light on its surface.

And, of course, water attracts wildlife. Animals and birds will come to drink. Create the right habitat and you may get frogs, newts and a world of insects, including damsel flies and dragonflies.

You can incorporate water in many ways, but a cheap option, costing you

How to create your own community garden: Sarah Eberle

around £50, is to buy a wooden half-barrel from a garden centre.

Once you've added the water, place water plants in the barrel. You can plant them in plastic baskets. But what we've done is to tie our waterlily to an old brick with string. This will keep it weighted down.

Wildflowers

Britain has lost 95 per cent of its meadowland since the Second World War. So in creating your Psalm 23 garden, why not incorporate a small area of meadow and help redress the balance?

You could put up a chalkboard and ask people to write down what wildlife they see every month. This will get people really interested and engaged, and it will help you see the difference the meadow area has made.

Somewhere to sit

Providing a seat in your garden enables people to sit down, relax and stay a while.

The most important thing to remember when putting a seat in a garden is that it needs to have a view. Look around, decide where you'd like to sit and put the bench or seat there.

There are lots of options for seating. If you're doing this at a church, you'll need to be sure to find out what is permitted.

But in the main, the restrictions are about what you can afford. You can buy a new bench, of course. If that's too expensive, though, look at what resources you have available. If you have recently cut a tree down, can you use the trunk as a place to sit? Or can you get something from a free site?

Download your free, easy-to-use guide to creating a Psalm 23-inspired community garden at: www.psalm23garden.co.uk

---

Plant list

Agrostis capillaris

Asplenium trichomanes

Carpinus betulus

Drosera rotundifolia

Juncus patens 'Carmen's Gray'

Pinus sylvestris

Rosa canina

Rosa pterocantha

Sedum anglicum

Selenium wallichianum

Vaccinium myrtillus

Viburnum opulus

Janet's story

'I had a severe fracture of my ankle a few years ago. The ankle didn't get set very well and it was in quite a mess. I was off work for months.

'It was really limiting. For the first three months I was just stuck in a chair in my living-room. It was difficult. You need a lot of patience, which I don't normally have.

'I missed doing things, although I do sew a lot, and I like hand-sewing, so that was very good in the sense that I could pass the time.

'I quilted Psalm 23. It is big enough to cover a normal double bed. At first, I was just putting scraps of material together; and on the reverse of the quilt was squares of white and squares of the colours from the front, and I thought white was boring really.

'Then we came upon a Japanese version of Psalm 23 [translated back into English]. That version is amazing. I have read through it so many times now. The words paraphrase the original version that we are used to, but they go deeper into that sense of rest and stillness and give you a new way of looking at the psalm.

'While I was sewing the words "efficiency through stillness of mind" it helped me gain patience in the middle of the situation I was in. It made me realise that I didn't need to fret. I had only been in my job for nine months and was looking at six months off. I realised that I didn't need to fret because God is with us.

'It gave me tranquillity. It was a sense of being held. It really helped my recovery. I needed the time to be physically, emotionally and spiritually renewed and refreshed, to recover. That happened through that time of sitting and hand-sewing. Hand-sewing has been the key to it. Sitting with needle and thread and patiently doing each stitch has been important. Stitching the word "rest" has enabled me to rest. "Do not fret" has enabled me not to fret.'

*Psalm 23 gave me a sense
of tranquillity in pain*

Community case study: *the lockdown garden*

During lockdown, the first community garden inspired by the Psalm 23 Garden was created outside St Mary's Church in Tadley, near Basingstoke. It became a symbol of hope for people across the community.

Community case study: **the lockdown garden**

A labyrinth of wild flowers, some espaliered cherry trees, and logs to sit on became the focal point of the local community.

'Lockdown felt like a cruel blow to our plans,' says minister, the Revd Gill Sakakini, 'but it's been a complete blessing, because it's given the garden a deeper meaning for the public.'

That meaning is hope. 'There was a sense in the community that something was happening,' she says. 'When we planted it, we could barely see the seeds. But week by week things grew and there was something that people could engage with when there was very little going on.'

Now, she says, the garden has become 'a focal point for the community'. 'My vision and my hope is that the garden will be a real place where people can connect with the natural world, a place that roots them, a place where they step outside their normal life and find what God has to offer,' she adds.

One of those for whom this is true is 48-year-old Julie Dollin. Shielding for many months due to health issues, Julie's first trip outside her house was to see the garden, named 23, after the psalm.

'I walked round the corner of the building and saw the garden for the first time, and it overwhelmed me,' she says. 'I was blown away by it.

'The garden gives me hope, a sense of well-being. Knowing I can come and sit here whenever life gets on top of me is great. It brings me closer to God.'

One of the key creators of the garden was Keith Gillings (67), a retired engineer with a passion for gardening.

Used to being busy and active, Keith found the lockdown especially hard. So, creating the 23 garden was 'an absolute godsend', he says.

'It was a fantastic time to be doing this,' he says, 'which may sound strange. But gardening really does restore your soul. It's a special garden to me. The bonus is that it's being well used.'

Anyone can use the garden at any time. But it's already being adopted for more formal purposes. It became part of a nature trail across the town, and is used for family events, prayer walks and outdoor services. There are also plans for the nearby school to use the garden.

'Despite lockdown, we found creating this garden easy to do,' says Gill. 'It's a fantastic way to connect with the community. It's a great opportunity.'